One of Us
Stories of Prostitution and Addiction

Cindy McMillion

For Lindsey and Wendy, with love

"I met this guy named Ray --- he was my pimp --- and I worked for him for a long time. He stopped having other girlfriends after a few years, and it was just me and him. I wasn't having to work the streets anymore. I haven't caught a prostitution charge in a long time, six or seven years, till now. Ray just wants me to stay in the house and not do anything. He takes the phone. He makes money working on cars, but lately he's said we need money. I went out and got a job at a grocery store and got hired and fired the same day because I didn't catch on to how to do things fast enough. I asked the manager could I take the steps home and study them and I'd know them by tomorrow, but she said, 'No, this is not going to work out.' I said, 'Are you kidding me? You just hired me three hours ago!' I'm a fast learner, but there wasn't any training. I don't want to wait tables because you don't make anything. I've done that before. They pay you, like, two dollars an hour and you're supposed to make it up in tips. But the only places I can get to in my part of town, they don't leave enough in tips. What am I going to do with a $20 paycheck?

"I can make four, five, six hundred dollars a day on the street. I know I can do that. I don't want to do it, but I don't have any other way to make money and we need it. I'm tired. I'm so tired. I don't want to leave Ray. I want to marry him, but he's used to being a pimp, so I don't know if he wants to get married. I know he cares about me though because when I get pissed off and disappear for days or weeks, he asks around and tries to find me. He wouldn't do that if he didn't care about me. I don't know what else to do. I don't know anybody but him. I don't have anybody else."

You have come by way of sorrow; you have come by way of tears...

- Julie Anne Miller

Introduction

In the spring of 2015, Sandra Ferrell invited me to sit around a dining room table with a small group of women who were working on rebuilding their lives after years of prostitution and drug addiction. I admit that I had no idea what to expect, but as each of the women in turn told their stories, I was struck by their courage, honesty, and determination. There were tears for the beatings and terror each had endured at the hands of their abusers --- often parents in the beginning and later pimps and johns --- but there was laughter as well. At one point in the evening, a spirited disagreement arose around the correct plural spelling of "whores." "It's h-o-s," insisted the woman to my right. "No, it's h-o-e-s," countered another. The peacemaker in the group finally put the debate to rest. "Let's just go old school," she said. "Hookers!" There was no veneer, no pretense, around the table that night. I came away knowing that I had been on holy ground.

Such was my introduction to the Community of St. Therese of Lisieux, a 12-step-based residential program offering help and hope to women willing to do the hard, hard work of forging new lives for themselves.

I'll begin with a collection of interview excerpts. Hearing these women's stories helped me better understand how early trauma can cause a person to be particularly vulnerable to predators and addictions. The accounts also opened my eyes to the brutality, despair, and horror that exist just below our radar. These women worked the same corners that I passed every day to and from work or errands or church. Of course I "knew" they were there, in the same sense that I was aware of robberies or car-jackings taking place daily in any city of size. But I had no idea how women ended up on the streets or what their lives were like. If I gave it any thought at all, I dismissed it with: "Why don't they put some clothes on and get a real job? They must like being out there. They must like having sex with different men every day."

God, forgive me. I didn't know.

I know that much of the material in the first section is difficult reading. There were times in the collecting and compiling of these accounts when I just had to step away and regroup; it is emotionally exhausting to be in the presence of such pain. But stay with it. Keep reading. There is light ahead.

Following the interview excerpts, you'll meet Sandra Ferrell, founder of the Lisieux Community. She will more fully describe the work that goes on there. Lisieux is only one of a handful of Memphis organizations that address the dual issues of prostitution and addiction, but it is the one with which I am most familiar. Others will be listed on the Resource page at the end.

I'll close with reflections from some of the Lisieux volunteers.

One final note: This work is dedicated to Lindsey and Wendy, two women who bravely walked away from the streets and worked very hard to conquer their demons and rebuild their lives. They were beautiful, kind, and true, but addiction is a vicious monster. Both women died of overdoses in the spring of 2018. Both were deeply loved and are greatly missed. The title of this work comes from a conversation I had with Wendy the day we met. She had been in the house only a few days and I, a volunteer driver and complete stranger, arrived to take her to an appointment. I will never forget her question to me: "Are you one of us?" she asked. I knew what she meant; I was neither a recovering addict nor a prostitute. But our commonalities went far deeper. I was just as vulnerable as she to the effects of trauma, abuse, and neglect. Her journey could have been mine. It could be anyone's. Would I have made the same choices if my circumstances had been like hers? I don't know. But her question will stay with me for a long time, and the only possible response --- the only answer I can give --- is, "I am a human being and a woman. So yes. Yes, I am one of us." We belong to each other.

Cindy McMillion
Memphis, Tennessee

The night is dark and I am far from home...

- John Henry Newman (1801-1890)

"The average age for getting pulled into trafficking is 13. I pictured young girls being snatched off the streets and forced into prostitution, but when I talked to the pimps, they told me that they don't need to do that when there are so many little girls who have such a deep need to feel loved and taken care of. All the pimps have to do is sweet-talk the girls, give them a compliment, and within seconds they can tell whether or not they have them. We as a community need to ask what has happened in these girls' lives to make them so vulnerable. So often it's a dad wound, a step-dad wound, or an uncle-wound that's a defining moment for them. Maybe they've been raped or hurt somehow and that's made them susceptible to men whose intent is to prey on them. For a lot of girls, the pimp is the first one who's ever made them feel special. They see him as a lover-boy or a dad-figure. If it were my first time to feel that important to someone, I'd probably go with him too. We need to ask, What is it about our society that perpetuates this tragedy? What can we do to prevent it?"

Jazmin Miller, Playwright / Author of *Thirteen*

"I was adopted when I was a baby, but my adoptive family used a lot of drugs, so by the time I was eight years old, I knew how to hide drugs in my vagina."

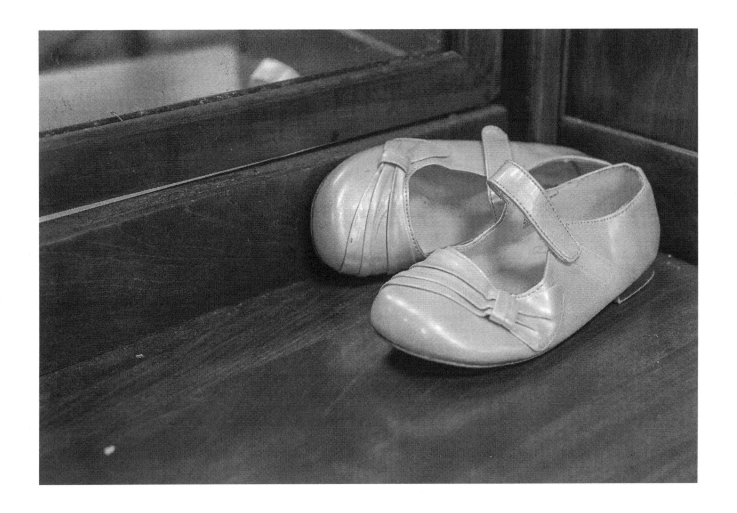

"I remember being in kindergarten or first grade --- I was very young --- and my mom came to school to pick me up. I was wearing a skirt that day, and I was coming down the slide. I was so excited to see my mom, but she was embarrassed and going off on me. She said, 'Why can't you slide down the slide ladylike? You have your legs open like a whore!' I was never able to be a child. I was always dirty and there was nothing I could do about it. That stuck with me. I was the whore. I was the one who was bad."

"When my brothers and I were kids and everybody got together for the holidays at my grandparents' house, they put out quilts and pillows and all the kids slept in the same room. I'm the only girl among my cousins, and one Christmas when we were there, my grandmother woke us up by jerking the blankets off of us. I've always been a heavy sleeper, so I don't know what happened, but when I woke up, my pants and panties were down to my ankles. I was made to feel very ashamed, like I was the one in trouble, and I don't even know what went on or who done it."

"My uncle abused me when I went to visit him and my aunt. They lived near the ocean, so we went swimming most days. Sometimes when we were playing in the water, my uncle would pick me up and throw me out a little further. One day when he did that, his finger went up inside me. And I --- I swam to the shore and I left him. In my mind, I was going, 'It was just an accident. Just an accident. He didn't mean it. They're Christians. He would never do that.' It made me feel so bad. But looking back on it now as an adult, he had to have known what he was doing. I've picked my kids up plenty of times and I've never touched them like that."

"Both my parents were alcoholics. My dad left when I was six months old, and my mom remarried when I was two or three. My real dad didn't come around much. When he did, he just threw money at us. He didn't pay child support, but he'd give my sisters and me fifty dollars to do with what we wanted. We thought that was just wonderful. To a kid, fifty dollars is a lot."

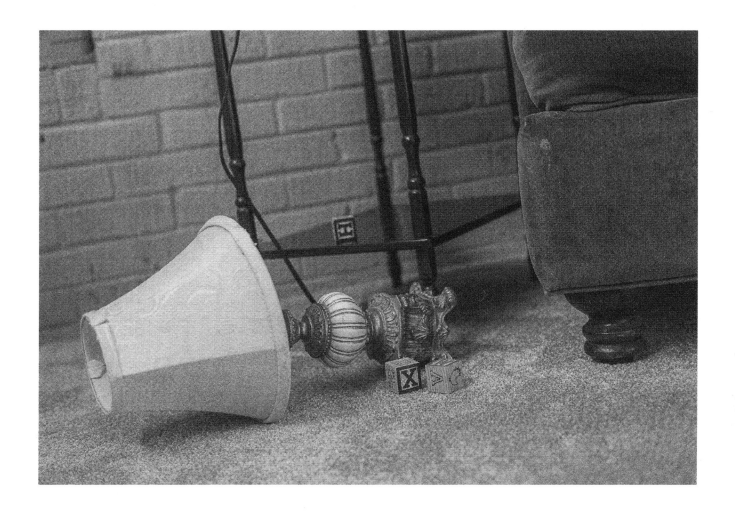

"My dad was addicted to alcohol and crystal meth. He and my mom got into terrible fights, and he was very abusive. Addiction changes you. You're not yourself. It's very powerful. When I say he was abusive, every tooth in my mom's mouth is screwed in. He broke bones, and he punched her in front of us. He punched her like a man. I remember screaming, 'Please don't hit my mom!' It was like I was in shock. This wasn't something I saw on TV. This was in my house."

"I was living at home with my mom and stepfather, and they were molesting me. All five of us children were physically abused by both of them. We got daily whippings that cut into our skin and made us bleed. After years of this, I ran away and was picked up by the police. An uncle (one who had been trying to get my parents to stop the beatings) came down to the police station and told them what was going on, but I was so afraid of my mom that I denied it."

"I grew up in another country, but my parents divorced when I was nine. After the divorce, my dad and I stayed in contact for a while but then lost touch. I don't know what ever happened to him. Alcohol is easily accessible where we lived, and I'd been drinking since sixth grade, so when my mom and I moved back to the States, that continued. I was smoking marijuana occasionally too, but when I got out of high school, got a job, and started working long hours and getting more and more exhausted and depressed, the drug use escalated. First there was cocaine, then Roxies (high-powered painkillers) and finally crack. Sometimes I'd get better for a while, but then I'd be really tired from the long hours at work, and I'd start back again. I ended up losing several jobs and tried twice to kill myself, but I couldn't quit using --- I didn't know how --- and I needed the drugs more and more just to get by. I started turning tricks in exchange for drugs."

"At some point my anger turned towards my mom for tolerating my dad's abuse, like: 'How can you?' She would call the military police and he would get thrown in the brig. She would place furniture against our door even when he was in the brig; that's how afraid she was. She was terrified to be with him, but afraid to tell him she wanted a divorce. Then he got a long overseas assignment, and that's when she divorced him.

"I still visited my dad after my parents divorced. I remember sitting at the table and him making me peppermint schnapps. I was ten years old then, and my alcohol of choice was Jim Beam. I never made mixed drinks. I guzzled Jim Beam, you know, trying to numb myself up at a very young age."

"As each of us children turned 13, my mom put us out of the house. I went to stay with my uncle. I could never focus in school. The teachers said I didn't do anything but daydream. After the ninth grade I dropped out, ended up on drugs, and got to the point where I was tempted to slit my wrists and commit suicide. I lived on the street, doing drugs, selling my body, homeless, and suicidal."

"When my mom started to date again after our parents divorced, us kids watched ourselves. We didn't have babysitters. Whenever she decided to go out, even if it was overnight, we were just... we were self-sufficient.

"The kids in the neighborhood thought we had the cleanest house anywhere, but my mom would come home from work and maybe find a popcorn seed behind the microwave. She would come in the living room and tell us, 'This house is a wreck', so we would go in the kitchen trying to figure out real quick what was wrong. And the more she thought of it, the more her anger would build. She would open up the cabinets and start throwing dishes at our feet and breaking them. And she was screaming the whole time, 'Clean up this fuckin house!' She'd go crazy."

"After my parents divorced, I moved in with my dad because he was diagnosed with cancer and there was nobody else who would help. I took care of him from the time I was 13 until he died two years later. After that, I lived with my mom, step-dad, and step-siblings for a while, but they didn't really want me there, so I left and moved out on my own."

"When we were teenagers, my brother introduced me to marijuana. We'd go out back, to the shed in the backyard, and he would roll a joint. I never talked a lot; I would be all up in my head, but my brother was hilarious. He was always trying to cheer up my broken soul."

"My older brother and I were very close. He was everything to me. I was always around him and his friends. He would say to them: 'You're my friend, but that's my sister. And I don't want to hurt you over her, so you just stay the fuck away from her. You're not going to touch her.' He was my protector."

"My older sister introduced me to methadone when I was 13. When I was 16, I got my own apartment, and people were in and out all the time; there were no rules. That's when I started using meth. As a senior in high school, I caught charges for credit card fraud, identity theft, and stealing from the gas station where I worked. I was convicted and received five years felony probation. That was in May. By June I was shooting up meth, cocaine, heroin, and anything else that a person could shoot up. My whole life was going downhill, and I lost my apartment. A drug dealer I hung out with introduced me to BackPage. You can find houses and cars and things like that on it like you can on Craigslist, but it's also used by prostitutes, pimps, and sex traffickers. The drug dealer and I got rooms in motels, and I put up an ad on BackPage for escort services. I did 'in calls' where the person would come to me and 'out calls' where I would go to them. One time when I was on an out call, I let the guy fix my shot (my dosage of drugs), and things happened that I had not signed up for. I used drugs intravenously for 5 years and prostituted for 4."

"After my mom remarried, the son of our new stepfather started molesting me. I don't know if I was his first victim or his only victim, but whenever it happened, I would think to myself, 'Scream. Say something. Do something.' But all I could think of was what my mom had gone through with my real dad --- all the abuse, all the screaming. My stepdad is a very good father, and my mom deserves to be happy, so I was protecting her and all of us. I thought, 'If she finds out, she'll divorce my stepdad, and then what are we going be faced with?' I was afraid she would find another man like my real father, somebody who beat us, so I never said anything. My stepbrother molested me for years. I was hurt, grossed out, disgusted, mortified, and angry. He raped me so many times. When my mom finally found out, she acted like I had asked for it, like somehow it was my fucking fault. And part of me thought maybe it was, like: 'Why didn't I scream out all those times?' I didn't scream because I was trying to keep our family from breaking apart again, that's why. When I was sixteen, I finally snapped. I said to myself: 'No one is ever going to protect me. I will have to protect myself. I refuse to live like this.' So I left home.

"A couple of years later, my stepbrother killed himself. From that time on, I felt his hands on me every single night till I was thirty. Every single night of my life, I would wake up and feel him touching me the way he had before. I felt like he killed himself so he could rape me for the rest of my life."

"I had my first consensual sex when I was 18 years old, and we got married a week later. He was very abusive. There was a lot of yelling and screaming, beating, and getting drunk. We weren't married for very long. I divorced him. Not long after that, my aunt's boyfriend raped me. He came to where I worked and asked me if I needed a ride home. He said he wanted to show me his house, so I went with him. It wasn't an attack; it was just forceful. It wasn't really rape --- but it was, if that makes sense. I didn't want to do it, but I knew I wasn't leaving until it happened. I was disgusted."

"I moved here ten years ago. The first guy who picked me up here drove me out to a field and said, 'You ever been fucked in the ass?' I said no, and he said, 'Well, that's how we do it in Memphis.' I don't want to stay here, I don't want to stay in this city, but I don't have family anymore."

"There was a lot of abuse, sexual and physical, from the time I was a child. As a teenager, I became an alcoholic and I smoked weed. I was in and out of bars and I wasn't even old enough to drink. I was always in a blackout, so I don't remember much."

"When I was thirteen, I went to live with a cousin, but I treated them like I was grown and I wouldn't listen to anybody. I dropped out of school and started prostituting. I've been arrested somewhere between ten and twenty times. One of the guys beat me so bad I lost an eye."

"I started dancing in strip clubs when I was 18, and that's where I met a pimp. He seemed like a nice enough guy until I started working for him; that's when I found out how violent he was. I met a trick and got hooked on ice (crystal meth), and that's what the pimp and I fought about the most: I wanted my drugs, and he wouldn't give them to me. We ate fast food, stayed in hotels, and had to see at least 10 tricks a day or we'd get beaten. All the money I made went to the pimp. If any of us were caught with any money, even a dollar, the pimp would have our heads. One night after I'd been with him for five months, we got into a big fight because I wanted ice, but he and his bottom bitch (second in command) were giving me spice (synthetic weed) instead so I would gain weight; I was getting too small. I told them I wanted to leave, and the bottom bitch literally beat the hell out of me. I ran out the door. I had been able to hide $100 in a cigarette case, so I got to the bus station and bought a ticket out of there. When I arrived at the bus station back home, there was a pimp waiting for me---a guy I had screwed over in the past. The pimp I'd been working for had called him and told him to find me. He snatched me from the bus station, and he and his bottom bitch held me hostage in a hotel for a week.

"I told them I was a wanted person and that if I didn't contact someone, the authorities would be looking for me, so they let me make a phone call. That was stupid of them, but I was able to reach my mom, and she got in touch with Homeland Security. I turned a trick for $80 and bolted out of the hotel door as soon as I was done. I ran to the nearest house, the person called a taxi for me, and I got to my mom's."

"My husband told me how much he hated me the day our first child was born. Second child, same thing. He was abusive verbally, cheated on me, and was physically abusive. I was doing anything and everything to keep him. It's like I had a sign on my back that said, 'Please hurt me.' I was attracted to abusive people. For ten years I begged this man to love me. My doctor prescribed Percocet when my second child was born, and when I took that, I knew I had met my best friend. My husband was not a pill popper, but he worked construction, so he got hurt a lot. I just waited patiently for him to get hurt, and then I took his pills. Eventually I had had enough and I left him. He never thought I would, because I'd dealt with his shit for years upon years upon years. By the time we divorced, I was taking Xanax for anxiety. My doctor prescribed them, but I didn't really care for them, so I would trade them for Lortabs. After a while, things escalated."

"I met a guy who gave me what I needed: attention and love, but it was sick, desperate love, the I-can't live-without-you type of love, like a serial killer. He was very protective; he'd beat people up over me. He was on all kinds of drugs: meth, crack, blow, everything. I'd never been around nobody that done shit like that. I didn't know what that did to a person, what the effects were. I didn't know. I just knew he was crazy as hell. I thought it was because he drank so much. He did bizarre shit like climb on top of the roof and punch holes in walls and beat the fuck out of me. He would get loaded and rape me in front of his friends. He was worse than my father was to my mom. He beat me bad. He beat me into drywalls. You could see my body print on the wall. He threw TVs. Then he would apologize and say he needed me, he loved me, and he couldn't live without me. I was with him for five years, until he went to prison for attacking me with a knife in front of some cops."

"I lost custody of my children because of all the chaos in my life. I fought for so long to get them back. I'd go to court, look up things in the law library, try anything I could, but then I realized I couldn't win. I felt defeated and just gave up. When I gave up, I gave up everything. I walked out. I went ten years homeless. Life had defeated me, and the streets --- the streets accepted me."

"I drank, smoked weed, took pills, and then went on to hard-core drugs. I was shooting up heroin and snorting cocaine. It made me sick at first, but then I got addicted. The only problem was, I couldn't afford to buy what I needed. One day on my way to the store to get cigarettes, a guy pulled up in a car and asked me to suck his dick for eighty dollars, so I did. It only lasted a minute or two, and I was on my merry way with eighty bucks. I got high as hell. I started walking all the time then.

"I made hundreds of dollars a day, but I was broke because I was doing 4 and 5 hundred dollars worth of drugs a day too. I was high 24/7 at this point. The only time I wasn't was when I fell asleep, and I hated falling asleep because I would always wake up in full detox."

"I stayed in abandoned houses ---I called them abandominiums --- and I didn't shower for months at a time. The tricks sometimes rent hotel rooms, so if I wasn't in a big hurry to get high or get my money back to my pimp, then I would slow down and take a shower. But even if I showered, I put the same clothes back on. I didn't have a place to keep anything. I got most of my clothes from the abandoned houses. I'd find things that would fit me, things somebody else had left, but they were disgusting. Oh my God, they were dirty and they stunk, but they were cleaner than what I had on my ass. I'd wear the same thing for months. Plus, as you can imagine, the clientele was not a very clean clientele; a lot of them were infested with bugs, like fleas, mites, and body lice."

"I worked around the clock. When I 'clocked out', I was in the dope house getting high. And then whenever my drugs were gone, I was back to work. I would be awake for months. I can't even tell you how long I was awake --- but months, months, without any real sleep."

"My very first pimp was my boyfriend, and he was addicted to drugs. He would tell me to go off and make money. He said that if I loved him, I would do it because we had to survive. So I did. With the next pimp, it didn't start off being sexual. It started off as 'I am your protector.' That's why I called him Daddy; he was going to protect me from the other people. I remember the first time he beat me up. He punched me so hard in my face that I busted out crying. It hurt, but it hurt more knowing that I had trusted him, and this is what he did.

"I think I made him feel bad, because he put his arms around me and he said, 'I'm so sorry. I will never do that to you again.' And he gave me extra heroin so I could numb up real good and not think about it. But of course that wasn't the last time. Each time he put his hands on me, it seemed to be easier for him to do."

"My first pimp told me to take money as payment, never drugs, and taught me how to 'walk the track', which is basically streetwalking. At my lowest point, I was smoking $400 worth of crack every day and making good money by working Backpage. Of course I had to turn it over to my pimp every day, but he gave me an allowance from it. Then one day I was robbed at gunpoint by a 'date', so I didn't have the money for my pimp and he kicked me out on the street. Working on my own, I could only make $20-60 per trick, but I needed a lot more for the drugs. That was a huge turning point for me. I gave up trying to live any semblance of a normal life and let go of any hope I had. All I cared about was crack, and I worked really hard every day to make enough to buy it."

"I got a job as live-in caregiver. The first person I worked for was fine, but when she was able to live on her own again, I had to find another place. A man hired me to take care of his disabled sister, but then he started coming on to me. When I refused him, he raped me and then told me to get out. I had nowhere to go, and almost no money. The man owed me $500 for the whole month, but he only gave me $50. He said that was all I was worth. There was a convenience store where I charged my phone, and for the next two days I called every single place in Memphis, every organization, but everywhere I called, there was either a waiting list or just a 'no.' I remember standing on the street in a heavy rainstorm, soaking wet, with no money and no hope."

"You never know who's going to pick you up or what they're going to want you to do. Every once in a while, you get in a car with somebody who's just not right and they want to kidnap and torment you. There's bad people out there, all over this area. There's serial rapists. I've been in situations where a man took me to graveyards and beat me and raped me. I've had to jump out of vehicles. I was in life or death situations on a regular basis. It wasn't just once or twice. It was daily, weekly. There was one guy who picked me up and put me at gunpoint. He told me he was taking me to this house, I'm going to make him money, and if I tried to escape, he was going to put a bullet in my head. I mean, you meet these people who... That's why I'm very good at assessing situations, because when I got in the car with somebody I had to figure out very quickly, by the time we'd gotten to the next red light, what the hell I'd gotten in the car with. I would try to see his eyes and know the situation because there was a lot of times that I'd have to bail. This guy took me off guard. He beat me and raped me. I don't know if you're just too high, it's too late, you're tired, or too fucked up --- but you can't escape every bad situation."

"There were guys in the hood who knew they could get me for $20 and businessmen in suits who'd pay hundreds of dollars. I was a hot little number, thin and good-looking, and I made money, a lot more than I could make with an eight-hour-a-day job. I've done detectives and police officers too. They never arrested me; I've never been to jail for prostitution. They picked me up, I did them favors, and they let me go. As a result of that, they didn't really fuck with me. They were cheap-paying though. I normally did it in the car, in the police car. One took me to an abandoned house. A detective. The people that are here to protect and serve? They take advantage."

"The majority of the business-suit type guys are married and they're looking. They're not happily married. They want some dirty sex that they're not getting from their wife or significant other and so they seek that out on the street, you know, and they get a fantasy fulfilled. Some of them fall in love. Some of them want to save you, but you're not savable at this point. You know, you just don't want to be saved."

"There are always people watching you when you're on the street. The only time you're not being watched is when a trick picks you up. The lookouts know when to expect you back at the house with their money, depending on where the trick takes you. So if you're not back on time, there's going to be a whole lot of questions, like 'Where you been and why have you been gone so long?' I can say, 'Because I was making more money. A john picked me up' and then they're happy with me. You have to prove that you have the money though. If I don't have the money, then I'm in a lot of trouble. A lot of trouble. Daddy would beat me up if I tried to keep any of the money I made, and then he'd send me right back out on the street looking like that. Black eyes, bruises, cuts, knocked-out teeth, a broken nose. One time I cuffed ten dollars and I got the shit beat out of me for doing that. And I cuffed the ten dollars in a body cavity. That's how much they looked for their money. They were looking in your body cavities. Any place a woman can hide something, they were looking.

"The worst thing you can do is stop and try to help somebody. We have quotas and we can't afford to waste our time talking. If we don't make as much as they think we should, we'll get beat up. There is always somebody watching."

"If you try to leave… you're brainwashed. You don't know to go get help. You don't think that way because you've tried to run away before. And when they find you it's a terrifying experience. You don't know if you're going to live through it, if it's ever going to stop."

"I stayed with this pimp, Dee, for ten years in a neighborhood off Summer Avenue, and I made a lot of money for him. Once, I got really pissed off at him and the other drug dealers there and I told them, 'You see all this money?' I had hundreds in my hand and I had it out like a fan, like this, and I said, 'You ain't getting a fuckin dime of it. I'm getting a new pimp. I'm getting a new drug dealer. Fuck all y'all. I'm done with y'all.' Dee started laughing and chasing me and say, 'Bitch, if you don't get in here with that money, I'm going to beat your ass right now in this road.' And then I started laughing because I needed that. I wanted to be needed. It didn't matter. If you were willing to beat me, I knew you wanted me.

"Dee was my protector. He didn't live at the trap house, but he was there every day and sometimes overnight. When he wasn't around, I was always afraid, but he was mostly around because I was a moneymaking girl. His wife loved me, his kids loved me, his girlfriends loved me. One thing I didn't like, though, was that there were times when he made me have sex with his friends to pay off some of his debts."

"When it was really cold or hot outside, you didn't get a lot of johns. But I was always very diligent because I didn't want to get my ass beat; I'd stay out there until I got somebody. And the more money I made, the more protection I got and the more praises I got. The other prostitutes --- I was one of the very few white girls out there --- were very racist. It would take three or four of them to come up with five dollars panhandling. And I would come in with hundreds of dollars, so you can imagine how they felt about me. They would try to rob me and beat me, so I needed that extra protection. I worked hard for it."

"After I finished high school and got married, life was great - for a while anyway. We had a house and things were going well. Then my husband got injured and had to resign from his job. Although he was able to get on disability, it wasn't enough to live on. That was the first thing. Then I got hooked on pain meds after some dental work. When I couldn't get them anymore, I started buying them on the street. I couldn't take just one or two. I had to have more than that. It got expensive, but I had to get that high. A friend told me heroin would be a lot cheaper, so eventually I broke down and tried it. For a long time I was just able to do it off and on, but then it got to a point where I had to do it every day. My husband got hooked on it too. I was so addicted that if I didn't have a fix first thing in the morning, I would be so sick I couldn't get out of bed. I was working at the time to supplement our income, but the drug use was interfering. I'd spend anywhere from forty to a hundred dollars a day on heroin. My husband was in and out of the hospital all the time with his health issues and I needed to be with him, so I resigned from my job. We got so behind on all our bills that we ended up living in our car. All we had was my husband's disability check. When the check came, we'd rent a hotel room for a couple of weeks, then the money ran out and we'd have to live out of the car. It was hard to keep clean, hard to keep clean clothes, and we didn't always have enough to eat. That went on for about eight months. It was so cold in the winter. My husband and I split up a couple of times during that period. That's where the prostitution came in. I never walked the streets. I just kind of hooked up with guys. It was more or less like boyfriend / girlfriend relationships --- and of course I'd have to have sex with them --- but I was just in it for the money. For survival. When I got tired of one guy, I found somebody else. Then my husband and I got back together. I knew I needed help. I needed to get off the drugs, so I told him I was going into treatment. All the other times he had followed me, but this time he didn't. I talked to him a few times on the phone, but then he didn't pay his phone bill and I couldn't get in touch with him anymore. Time went by and then one day I got a call that he had died. I don't know how to deal with the guilt and the grief. I really don't. Some days it will be so bad. It just grips me. And then some days I'm okay. I sleep a lot, trying not to think about it. I'll tell myself, you know, that I did the very best that I could with what I knew at the time, but sometimes the grief seizes me and it's just hard to get away from."

"If you see a guy with a sign at an intersection that says he's hungry, he's probably just hungry for heroin. He may be hungry for food too, but he's really looking to get his next fix. That's what the guys do. They panhandle. They hold signs. The women walk the street because sex sells."

"I can't tell you the number of women and men I watched die in the streets. I've seen people overdose. I've watched people get stabbed to death. There was gunfire on a daily basis. It was just... you heard it all the time, so you just weren't even afraid no more. It was just life."

"I was in a long-term relationship, but it ended and I had to start over and support myself. I found jobs, but the pay was low and it was extremely hard work. Finally I couldn't find a job anymore. I lost two apartments, the unemployment money stopped, and the only way I could make ends meet was prostitution. I had an acquaintance who offered me money and introduced me to other men, so I slept with him in exchange for the contacts. I got to keep my money. I didn't like it, but I had to have something to live on. I did that for 2 years."

"Rape happens all the time out here. The other girls and I would watch out for each other. Like, if they know somebody is a rapist, they might say: 'Watch out for a silver SUV.' And you do watch out for it, but then you also think: Maybe they're telling me to stay away from it because they don't want me to get that money. They want to do that person and get the money."

"I tried to stay on the outskirts of the hood at nighttime because at night, the hood will attack you. The younger gangs, you know, if they want to have sex with you they get between 10 and 15 men to chase one of us down in the streets. One night when that was happening, I was lucky enough to get away, but the girl I was with wasn't. They caught her and held her face in a puddle of water while they raped her. She ended up getting pneumonia. It was a brutal rape, a brutal attack."

"One day my pimp's house got shot up. I was in there getting high and a bullet nicked me. The wound got infected, I had surgery, and I ended up spending months in the hospital. I went from there to a treatment facility, and I managed to get a year, but you know the whole time I'm doing this, my mind is still on my Daddy, like: 'I bet he wonders where I'm at. I bet he's thinking about me.' All that's far from the truth, I'm sure, but I missed him and I thought about him and I actually loved him. I left recovery to go back to him."

"I've been a prostitute for so long that I don't even know how to have a relationship with a man. It's like: I learned how to add and subtract, okay, but I never learned how to multiply. It's not that I *can't* learn how to multiply, it's just that I never learned how. I have to learn how to have a relationship. I have to unlearn a lot of bad skills."

"Ten years of walking the track and I'm wore the hell out. Literally. My body is exhausted."

"I hate men. No, I don't hate them --- I love them --- but they scare me. Maybe they're innocent, but I can't click that off in my brain. It's just there permanently. And so, as a result, I end up getting high over it."

"All my life, I've wanted someone to love me, but I confuse love with sex because that's what came first: it was the sex. Love never really came, so I just assume that when someone loves you, they're going to hurt you. Men have been touching me since I was a baby and so I thought maybe I exuded --- that it was my fault somehow; I made men want to have sex with me. You know, if I saw a little girl getting raped, I would try and kill the man, but for me, when I'm being raped, somehow it must be my fault."

"When I started trying to protect myself, it was to run away from home. And then I ran to men who hurt me worse than my family did. I'm missing teeth because of men beating me and punching me in the face."

"I was actually numbing my whole life. When I first started getting high, it was because I didn't want to be reminded of the pain I had experienced. As early back as I can remember, there was pain. So I numbed that. And I lost my kids. That was the biggest pain I couldn't numb. I couldn't block it out."

"We were little girls with the same Cinderella dreams like other little girls, and then life happened. You don't know how you're going to handle a situation until you're in that situation. I've seen all kinds of things, you know. And people handle things different. I've seen people get raped and never get high. I'm not them though. I'm me, and this is my journey."

The End of the Beginning

"In the last place I lived, I was accused of stealing $20 and almost got killed over it. When that happened, I ran. I left behind everything I owned and called my sister. She took me to rehab---that was two months ago---and then my mom found the community living program I'm in now. I don't mind talking about this because I want people to realize that you can't tell what a person is dealing with just from how they look on the outside. You can't tell what people have been through. But no matter what it is, no matter what you've done, there is help out there somewhere if you want it badly enough."

"Finally, I got a call from a shelter, and they said a bed had opened up. I got there as fast as I could and stayed for 3 months. I was so grateful to have somewhere to go. Being there helped me forget for a while what I had gone through. While I was at the shelter, a woman told me about the program I'm in now. It sounded too good to be real, so it was a while before I contacted them, but she kept encouraging me, so I finally applied and got in. That was seven months ago.

"Becoming homeless was the major turning point in my life. Because of that journey, I've learned what it is to count my blessings and to be grateful. When I get in a bad place, I remember it was by the grace of God that I found this home. I want to get on my feet, complete this program, and try to do something to help other people. That's my dream."

"I was still huffing inhalants and drinking, and I needed help. My parents found a community living program for me. I remember my mom crying when we got the email that I was accepted. It was 3:42 in the afternoon. I'll never forget that. My parents brought me to the program that weekend, and I've been in it for six months. I was suspicious and so scared when I first got here. I couldn't believe people would do this for me without expecting anything back."

"I'm 20 years old, but I feel 40. My life is so different now because I have love. Real love. I don't have to second-guess the decisions of the people who work here because they have my best interests at heart. I'm in an environment where there is no chaos, no pimps, and no hoes. My hope for the future is that someday I can give back by helping some other crazy 20 year old."

"Six months ago, I saw a brochure about a community living program. I called and was accepted. My life has changed tremendously since that time. I still have struggles, but I have my sanity back. I'm learning how to live again, but in a different way than I ever have. When I feel like giving up, I talk to a staff member or one of my peers. I have hope that I can hold on to now, hope to get me through."

"In July, I will have been in this program for a year. It's been good for me. It's been hard, but good. Living in community is a big adjustment, because you know we don't all clean the same way, we don't all cook the same way, and we all have different reactions to things. I'm learning how to take better care of myself now: physically, mentally, emotionally, and spiritually. I'm trying to get my feet back on the ground, get a job, and build up some savings for when I eventually move out. I'm very thankful for Lisieux. It's made such a big difference in my life. Without it, I don't know where I would be. The most important thing I've learned is to lean on God, to trust God, to quit trying to do things my way. I still have trust issues, but I pray. When I have a problem, I say to God, 'Okay, I'm going to trust you to take care of this.' Before, it was hard for me to do that."

"I was on felony probation, and I was supposed to report to my probation officer once a month, but there were a lot of gaps in there when I didn't report for a long time and I'd have to go to jail for a few weeks. Sometimes, to avoid jail, I'd check into rehab, but I didn't stop using. Then in February I overdosed and was really, really sick. When I checked into rehab that time, I knew I had to make some major changes. If I continued the way I was going, I was going to die. I knew I had to stay in rehab. If I went out again, I would use. That's why I was never able to be a drug dealer. I wouldn't have made any money; I would have done the drugs myself. So I stayed, and that place saved my life. I couldn't have left anyway. I didn't have anywhere to go---not anywhere good. After 5 weeks in rehab, the case manager looked for a place for me and found a community living program in Memphis."

"I don't want to set my goals too high right now --- I have to finish this program first---but one day I'd like to work with children as a social worker or as a drug counselor. My brother's friend's daughter was really bad into drugs. I talked to her about the rehab I went through, and now she's turned her life around, so I feel like I've already made a difference with somebody. I think because of what I've been through, I can help other people in the same situation. I want to show kids and teenagers that there's a different way, that there's a way out. I want to give back. I don't think God created me to die a junkie."

"If I could help another woman who's been through some of the things I've been through and let her know that God will solve all her problems if she lets him, that would bring me so much... I'd know that my pain, my life pain, would have been worth going through."

"Did I like prostitution? No, but I knew I could use my body, my sex, at a very young age. I knew what men wanted. And they were going to take it, so I might as well make money doing it."

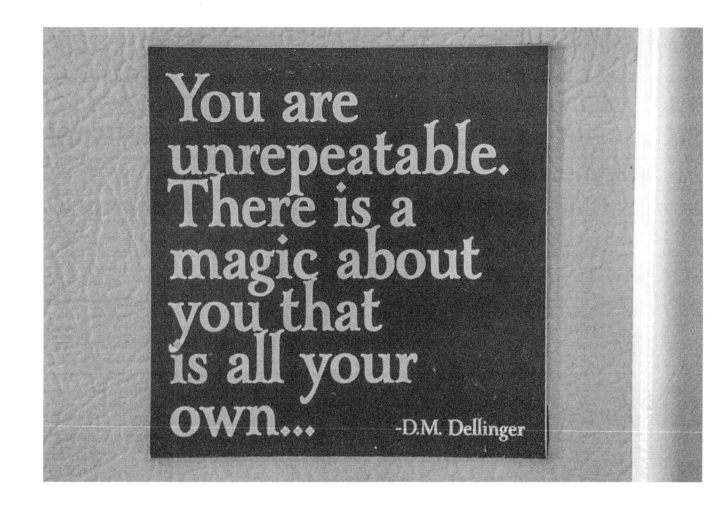

"I want to be courted. I want to be loved. I want to be in a relationship with someone who doesn't think that all I have to offer is sex."

"I'm exhausted, but I'm learning to love life one more time. I'm happy, I'm laughing. I've been clean for a few months now, but it's not a quick fix. It's not. One day I want to die and the next day I don't. It's a gradual thing, you know. It gradually happens over time, so I'm learning how to have hope. I'm learning to do this one day at a time."

"My biggest fear is, What happens after this? Will I relapse? Will I have it together? I can't tell you I will never get high again. I can't. I made promises before that I would never relapse again, and then I did. I'm not going to make any more empty promises."

"I have no idea what the future holds, but it's very scary for me. I'm having to learn all new rules. At least with my pimp, I knew what was expected of me. I knew what to do. I knew what I'd get in trouble for and what I wouldn't. In recovery, everything is new. It's really hard work."

"I have flashbacks about all the years I was on the streets. They're so real. It's like I was in a war. I survived a war. This is the first time I've wanted to live. Before, I didn't feel like living. I didn't feel like trying. Now I do."

"I like to think of myself as a victor --- instead of poor, pitiful, sad and depressed --- because I'm not a sad person. I'm not a depressed person. I'm a very happy energetic woman and I am so proud of the things that I have overcome in my life.

"I'm a warrior. Put that down. Call me a warrior."

The Community of St. Therese of Lisieux

Sandra Ferrell, President and Executive Director
lisieuxcommunity@gmail.com

"When I was small, Mother left me in the care of a man and his wife while she and my older siblings picked cotton on the couple's farm. It's how she made money for our school clothes all the time we were growing up. In the mornings when Mother dropped me off with them, she would tell me, 'Behave and do what the man says', never imagining that anything bad would happen. She trusted these people; they were part of the church that my daddy pastored. But something bad DID happen. Over the next two years, the man sexually abused me. I never told my parents about it because I was too young to know it was wrong and I'd always been taught to obey. That early abuse set me up for more abuse later on. I was molested again when I was eight and another attempt was made when I was twelve. I didn't say anything to Mother or Daddy those times either. I thought adults were always right, and if there was an issue, then I must be the one at fault. I continued to mature physically and mentally, but because of the abuse, parts of me were stuck at different ages.

"My life gradually became unmanageable. By the time my own kids were 12 and 16, they were maturing past me emotionally. I no longer knew how to handle dealing with them, so I took them for counseling. The counselor said, 'And we can help you too.' I said, 'No I'm fine.' Fortunately, she didn't laugh at me. She put me in the hospital for an intensive week, and over the next year, I began to deal with the pain caused by the early abuse. I began to grow up."

"Then, one Sunday I was in church when a woman came to speak about a program she had started in Nashville for women coming out of prostitution and drug addiction. An audience member asked how many of the women in the program had been sexually abused. I heard her say: Almost all were abused before they were 11 years old, and certainly all were abused after the prostitution began. Suddenly I realized I could have ended up on the streets. That could have been my life. Thankfully, I had a family who held me close and that didn't happen --- but it could have, under different circumstances.

"That day, the idea for the Lisieux Community was born, a ministry that provides housing and help for women who have been trafficked and who want a different future for themselves. It's intense work, both for them and for the staff, but it's important. These women could have been me. They could be any of us."

"Whether we use the word trafficking or prostitution doesn't really matter because it's the same kind of pain. It usually begins with a girl being seduced by a man who's older than she is. The girl is flattered because she's getting attention from an older man; it makes her feel special. He will "groom" her for several weeks and then eventually he will say something like, 'You love me don't you? I need you to do me a favor.' And she'll say, 'Anything. What can I do?' He'll say, 'I've got a friend coming and he wants a lady to sleep with him, you know, to make him feel good. And he'll make you feel good. Will you do that for me? I'd really appreciate if you would.' From there it very quickly escalates to: 'You owe me. Think about all the things I've done for you. You need to do what I ask you to.' If the woman balks or tries to leave, she ends up getting beaten. She then feels that she has no options."

"I believe that women get there one of three ways One is, it's a family that probably doesn't have the skills to raise children because they've never resolved their own issues. The children are very vulnerable and seek the attention wherever they can get it. The second way is a family that's pretty healthy, but something traumatic happens to them. Maybe Dad loses his job or maybe a parent dies, and the children struggle to figure out how to take care of themselves. Again, those children are vulnerable and it's easy for somebody to prey on them. The third way is when a woman doesn't have job skills and something happens to the relationship she's in --- divorce or death --- another man may step in and say that he wants to take care of her. That may lead to her being used, and then once she's in that situation, no matter what age or how much schooling she's had or how many jobs she's held in the past, when she tries to get away, she suffers consequences that are very severe.

"One lady that I know of had breast cancer after being in recovery. She lost her hair, and that was the first she realized that she had a roadmap on her head. She'd been beaten so many times. Why beat someone on the head? Because it doesn't show. The hair will cover it. After a beating, the woman is made to put her head under cold water to make the bleeding stop, then she has to go back out and sell herself again to another man. It's a horrible thing to think about."

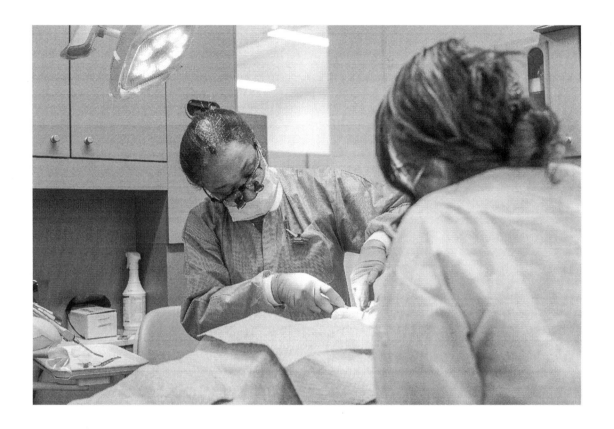

"We have served women from 18 to 62 years of age. Some have not been out as long as others. Some women have had work experience before they started out on the streets and so they have some skills. When they come to us, we began to assess what needs to be done. They usually have not been to the doctor for a long time, so we set them up with a medical professional to see that their physical needs are addressed. We take them to a mental health clinic to make sure that whatever meds they're on are still appropriate. Sometimes while a woman is here, her diagnosis will change because she begins to be healthier and not have the same symptoms she did when she first came. Mental health needs are addressed on an ongoing basis. Then there's dental care. Some drugs will cause dental health problems, but the other issue is that when you're living on the streets it's very difficult to take care of your teeth appropriately. There are usually lots of things that need to be corrected when somebody comes in."

"The women are responsible for taking care of the house, for keeping it clean and uncluttered. They prepare menus and shopping lists and go and buy the groceries for the house. Things that a lot of people take for granted, but if we haven't had the opportunity to practice them, then they're not comfortable for us. We do community service as well because when you are receiving help, it feels better if you can give something back. Right now we have a friend who works with an emergency shelter, and the day after they host people for the night, she brings the sheets and our women launder them. At one time we were working in a community center serving meals, and we hope to do that again."

"After her first three months here, sometimes a woman will choose to go through HopeWorks, a 13-week personal and career development class offered in Memphis. We've had some women who have taken classes at the local community college and gone straight into a job. The path they take depends on what they want to do with the rest of their lives. Our goal is to offer a safe and supportive home for up to two years. We could probably teach life skills in six months, but it takes longer than that to really solidify them. Otherwise, when you get out there to try this different way of living, you often fall back in with people who are making unhealthy choices. We prefer that women take time to encounter their problems and have support from other people in the group to address their issues. It's hard sometimes when a woman leaves before the two years is up and you know she doesn't really have a lot of skills."

"Seeing how other women are working their program changes the life of each person who is here. It changes my life and the lives of our volunteers as well."

"We can have up to five women at a time because in Memphis no more than five unrelated adults can live in a house that is zoned residential. You would have to be zoned commercial and we intentionally don't want a commercial place. We don't want a place that feels like a business because when people leave here the goal is to be in a home of their own."

"We get referrals a variety of ways: Homeland Security, recovery and rehab centers, our sister organization in Nashville, and crisis stabilization units, among others. We ask that a woman interested in coming to us first go through a 28-day program at a recovery center. Coming here straight off the streets would be very difficult. Being in a recovery facility for 28 days gives the women a foundation to build on."

"Women may choose to leave before the two years is up. For some, it's because they're convinced they've done all they need to do. The three-month mark is often when people begin to think, 'I got this.' Sometimes they go out and relapse, and sometimes they come back to us. We welcome that as long as they're still willing to do the work. Some people have obligations to children or adults in their family --- or they believe they have obligations --- and they need to get a job and go on. Those people usually keep in touch with us in one way or another. And so it's not that they quit working on their recovery; it's that they do it in a different way."

"We had to ask one woman to leave because she had men and drugs in the house. She started yelling and screaming and throwing things around, and I called the police. A year and a half later I got a call from her, and she said, 'Ms. Sandra, I wanted to say I'm sorry for the way I behaved at your house.' I said, 'Wow, that means a lot to me. Thank you for calling. Where are you now?' She had a job working 30 hours a week at a supermarket. She was also cleaning a church and living in a house they provided. She said, 'Miss Sandra, this wouldn't have happened if you hadn't did what you did to me.' And I thought it was funny that she said 'did what you did to me' rather than 'what you did for me.' About six months later I got another call from her saying, 'I'm in my own apartment. If you've got somebody that moves out and needs an apartment to share, I'll be happy to share.' She also said, 'I'm working 50 hours a week now as a cashier at the supermarket.' So we don't always feel like we can keep in touch, but getting the text about someone finishing their GED or getting those calls from her --- it's pretty cool. There are others I keep in touch with too."

"Through a grant, we got a house that had been foreclosed on but was still in good shape. We rehabbed it with a portion of the grant money and then furnished it in large part with donations from the 12-step community. We bought some appliances, and a volunteer group built a shed and pavilion for us. It costs us about $5000 a month to operate. The Church Health Center provides free medical care for our women. There have been some other professionals --- dentists, for example --- who have donated services, but you can't call on the same people all the time."

"By the time a woman leaves our program, we hope she will be able to live life on life's terms, to borrow a 12-step phrase. We hope she will have learned how to live so that when things get difficult, she can make it. Our goal is to help her build a really good foundation so that she knows how to navigate problems and doesn't relapse the first time something difficult comes along. We know that things are always going to be hard; when somebody leaves here, we're not expecting it to be easy. We're expecting them to have the tools to be able to deal with life."

"We ask the women to put 40 percent of earnings into savings, because when you move out it's going to take about 40 percent of your salary to pay rent and utilities. If you're used to not living with that 40 percent already, then that gives you a good basis for going forward. When a woman completes the program then, she has savings to either help put a down payment on a house or pay the utility and rent deposits to get settled in a place."

"Every one of our residents is dealing with addiction and prostitution at some level, but everyone's story is different. That's why, when I show visitors through the house, our first stop is in the kitchen. Each kitchen cabinet has a different knob on it, as a visual reminder that every person who participates in the program --- whether as a resident or as a volunteer --- is unique and should be treated that way."

"The hardest thing with almost any nonprofit is funding. I fill a lot of roles in both the oversight and daily operation of the residence because we haven't conquered the funding challenge. We need more staff, but we can't hire without a larger financial base. At one point I was making myself sick by not taking time to rest. Now, I have learned to call on volunteers to take the women to their various appointments."

"I have a volunteer who comes on Tuesday and writes thank you notes. That doesn't sound like a lot, but it's huge to have somebody keeping up with those. We consider it an honor when individuals or groups give of their time and skills. We appreciate what they do. The other night when I took the women to church, Kristin and Margaret sat on either side of them. It was wonderful to be given that respite. We also have a group of ladies from that same church who come once a month to share a meal and offer friendship. It's the relationships that mean so much. It's hard for me to deliver that relationship at the same time that I'm delivering things they don't want to hear. Because of growth areas, you sometimes have to be the hard mom. I did my own work first, but then I also went through it with my kids. I had to do some hard stuff with them, and I see what remarkable people they are now."

"And then too, I've had to learn how to let go of my ideas about success. Anytime a woman chooses to leave, I remind myself of St. Paul's words: He says that some of us plant, some of us water, and some of us get to see the harvest. If I plant, I can't feel like I failed because I don't see results. Or if I water and I don't see the harvest, it doesn't mean the program wasn't successful. It took a lot of work for me to come to that understanding in my own mind."

"Early on, I would have said that the most rewarding aspect of this work was knowing the wonderful women who are out there. But now I would have to say it's the 'aha!' moments, whether mine or someone else's. Once we understand one thing, it opens us wider to understand the next thing and the next. We're not so scared anymore. For me, when I see a bit of progress, I know the next step is possible."

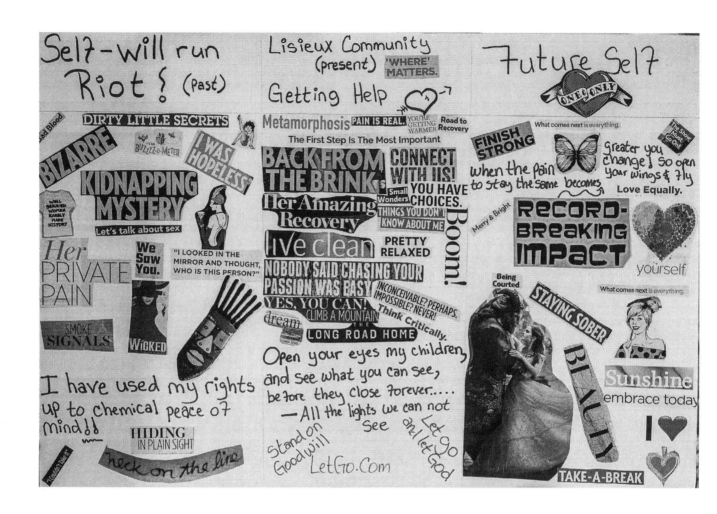

Wendy's vision board

Reflections from Lisieux Volunteers

In my time volunteering to drive Lisieux residents to appointments, I have been impressed with the determination they show. Imagine leaving, as an adult, whatever living situation you have, all the people with whom you have been associating, and at the same time taking every step to beat whatever addiction you might have. Even though their situations may have been deeply unhealthy before, it still takes tremendous courage to step away and enter a completely new environment. I always pray for each new resident of the community house especially as she settles in to her new life, knowing that every bit of her might be longing for a return to what is familiar, even if that situation is damaging.

- Nancy

How profoundly can lives be changed through simple food and fellowship around a dinner table? I've seen it firsthand. I believe as a volunteer that I make a small difference, but larger than that is the way that I have been humbled and spiritually enriched through my friendships with the ladies of the Lisieux Community.

- Sarah

Before volunteering with the Lisieux Community, I had no idea how women become entangled in the cycle of prostitution and its accompanying difficulties. Learning about the journeys of these women has been eye-opening. It is so compelling to offer them companionship as they walk in a new direction.

- Margaret

When I started volunteering I had no idea how I would feel two years out, how I would be changed. I never knew how deeply I would feel toward the residents; that I would fall in love with them and that I would have my heart broken by them on more than one occasion. I hope that my time spent with them has added value to their journey, because I know beyond a shadow of a doubt that I have been changed. I know that in order to connect with someone, we must allow ourselves to become vulnerable. Being vulnerable is a tough one for me, but they are worth it! We are women taking care of women and, as Ram Dass says, "We're just walking each other home." I love that quote; I believe that is what we are doing at Lisieux.

- Tracy

Volunteering at Lisieux to take dinner to the residents monthly has provided an opportunity to serve and to be in community with the residents. It has deepened my view of Christian love and serves as a strong reminder that whoever we are and whatever our path, we are all God's children. So thankful for Lisieux.

- Mary

When I first joined the ladies at Lisieux for a dinner I didn't know what to expect and I guess it surprised me that they looked like me. Any one of these women could be my sister, mother, daughter, or - if my circumstances had been different - me. Like all of us, they were looking for friendship, family, community, stability, and healing.

Hearing the ladies' stories makes me very aware that I have been extremely sheltered, and the things that I consider trauma in my life are nothing compared to the trauma in their lives. It is eye opening and helps me to be more patient with others in general – realizing that there is always something deeper than what we see on the surface. When we meet someone, we don't know their history, we don't know why they are the way they are or why they say and do the things they say and do. By recognizing that there is much that we don't know, we allow ourselves to be open to differences, to be more understanding, patient, and welcoming.

And it's not just the ladies from Lisieux that have touched me during this journey. Meeting and getting to know the other volunteers at a deeper level has truly enriched my life.

Spending time together in a place like Lisieux allows us or even requires us to be vulnerable and real in order to embrace one another. This experience has stretched me as a person, all for the better.

I don't have the means to make significant monetary gifts but I can cook dinner, I can be present, I can hang out with the girls, I can laugh and give big hugs.

I am so very thankful that the ladies feel comfortable enough to share their stories and their lives and that they somehow reap benefits from our time together. I am so very thankful for their gifts of trust and friendship. Knowing them continues to make a huge positive impact on me.

- Kristin

Church of the Holy Communion is privileged to serve as the spiritual home base for several members of The Lisieux Community. The women of Lisieux are not guests at Holy Communion, but a part of the whole. All of us have been changed by being in relationship with each other, despite all of the variations in the stories of our lives, and the distinctions between "them" and "us" have melted away. This is what the Kingdom of God looks like.

The Reverend Alexander H. Webb II
Rector, Church of the Holy Communion
Memphis, Tennessee

RESOURCES

Tennessee Human Trafficking Hotline
1-855-558-6484

Restore Corps (contact point for West TN)
https://www.restorecorps.org

Community of St. Therese of Lisieux
https://lisieuxcommunity.org

A Way Out
https://www.ccvmemphis.org

Thistle & Bee Enterprises
http://www.thistleandbee.org

HopeWorks
https://www.whyhopeworks.org

About the author

Cindy McMillion is a writer and photographer living in Memphis, Tennessee. She shoots regularly for the Lisieux Community, the community breakfast at St. Mary's Episcopal Cathedral, Church of the Holy Communion, Caritas Village, and other non-profits. From 2014-2017, she interviewed and photographed a wide variety of Memphis residents, culminating in the *Connecting Memphis* exhibit at Christian Brothers University. The pieces from that exhibit are now part of the university's permanent collection and are available for loan to other institutions.

Cindy may be contacted at cindymcmillionphotography@gmail.com

99796036R00063

Made in the USA
Columbia, SC
13 July 2018